SURVIVALIST FINANCE

Maximise your chances of survival with minimum effort and money

Renaud Gaucher

SUMMARY

INTRODUCTION

I want to maximise my chances of survival and the chances of my family in the event of an economic collapse while I am lazy and not rich. How to do that?

I asked myself this question and I used the fact that I studied finance and that I have people in my family who have developed a high level of autonomy to answer.

In this book, we will discover my answers. The content of this book is not a financial advice. you have to do your own research. But this book will give you food for thought as you try to make better decisions for yourself and to protect your family.

In the first chapter of the book, we will look at the central concepts of survivalist finance. In the second chapter, we will look at how to develop a personal survivalist finance when living sedentary. In the third chapter, we will look at how to develop personal survivalist finance when living nomadic and/or preparing to flee a country, whether for war or other reasons.

CHAPTER 1: CENTRAL CONCEPTS OF SURVIVALIST FINANCE

Economic collapse

There are many reasons that can lead to a major change in our daily lives, a breakdown in normality: economic crisis, unemployment, war, lack of natural resources, climate change, divorce, death of close relatives, etc. Not all of these reasons necessarily lead to economic collapse, but in most cases there is an economic collapse, i.e. a major reduction in production activities and consequently in the standard of living. This is one of the two reasons why the notion of economic collapse is central to survivalist finance. The other reason is the link between personal finance and surviving economic collapse.

Basic needs

Basic needs are the level of comfort we want to try to maintain even in the face of economic collapse.

This level varies from person to person. A person living on the equivalent of less than 2 dollars a day in a poor country will not consider the same level of comfort as a rich person in a rich country as basic needs.

Talking about basic needs rather than money is important from a survivalist perspective of personal finance, because money is just a means to acquire what we need to satisfy our basic needs and it is not the only means, it is also possible to produce what we consume. This is what most of humanity has done for most of human history.

Operating in a society where money is exchanged for goods and services, we forget that money is only a means to satisfy our needs. This idea may seem to conflict with the idea of survivalist finance, but we will see that it does not in the course of the book.

In their book "Rues barbares" ("Barbaric streets"), Piero San Giorgio and Vol West, two eminent French-speaking survivalists, give a list of 7 pillars of survival. These 7 pillars are:

- Water

- Food

- Hygiene and health

- Energy

- Knowledge

- Defence

- Social link

They provide with this list a basis for defining basic needs. We could add an eighth pillar, housing, which is implied in the list of survival pillars. We will come back to the definition of basic needs when we look at how they can be met from the perspective of survivalist finance.

Resilience

Resilience is the ability to survive and live in a situation of economic collapse, where an economic collapse can be characterised as a situation where money is no longer available to buy life-sustaining goods such as clean water, food or, in countries with cold winters, heating.

I talk about sedentary resilience when a person lives sedentary and nomadic resilience when a person live nomadic. Sedentary resilience is less complicated than nomadic resilience, but a sedentary person, in some cases such as fleeing from war, may be forced to move from sedentary to nomadic resilience.

Asset security

The security of an asset is the most important characteristic of an asset. When we own something, the first thing to think about is how to avoid having it stolen.

The security of assets varies according to two characteristics: the type of asset and who is responsible for the security.

The issue of security varies according to the type of asset and we can make a typology of assets according to the security issues they generate. In this typology, there are two types of assets: material assets and pseudo-material assets (I wrote "pseudo-material", because even the most immaterial assets have a material reality). Let us give some examples of these different types of assets and some explanations.

Examples of material assets are: personal housing, land, forest, vegetable garden, cans of food, water supplies, chairs, cash, housing that is rented to someone else. In these material assets, there are assets that one uses to satisfy one's needs directly and assets from which one earns income that can then be used to satisfy one's needs.

Examples of pseudo-material assets include bank deposits, stocks, bonds, ETFs or financial instruments designed to closely replicate changes in an index, and crypto-assets.

The money one has in notes or coins is a material asset, because one holds the notes and coins in one's hand. Money in a bank account is pseudo-material: one does not have the notes and coins that it could represent in one's hand, but there are servers where the information of the existence and the sums deposited in the account exists.

In terms of both material and pseudo-material assets, there are two main types of security: the security provided by others (states, banks, security companies, etc.) and the security that we provide ourselves. Generally, there is a mixture of the two with a more or less strong dominance of the security provided by others.

If we go back to the examples of money and bank accounts, we can see that states and banks try to guarantee cash that is not counterfeit money, that states normally have a police force that tries to dissuade this cash from being stolen from us, and that we try to ensure that this money is not stolen from us, for example by carrying small amounts of money with us that limit the risk of theft.

With regard to our bank account, the bank has a duty to secure the amounts deposited and the access to those amounts, however, this security comes at a price, which is that the bank may not allow us to access our money, even if we comply with its protocols. The bank may go bankrupt and not return our money. It can also be ordered by a government to block our access to the bank account as was done in Canada against people who were accused of rising up against the curtailment of civil liberties.

Put another way, the more the security of our assets depends on others, the more those others can dispossess us of our assets.

The two major dimensions we have described for any asset (asset type and security type) allow us to create a matrix in which any asset can be described. We will call this matrix the asset security matrix. It is as follows:

Asset Security Matrix

	Impersonal defence (by others)	Personal defence (by oneself)
Physical assets		
Intangible assets		

This matrix allows any asset to be described according to its degree of materiality and the degree of personal defence it allows.

Asset liquidity

In traditional finance, asset liquidity is the ease with which a financial asset can be bought or sold quickly, without major impact on its price.

In survivalist finance, the liquidity of an asset is the ease with which it can satisfy a basic need. For example, a tin can is more liquid than money because it can be consumed immediately, whereas it will take some time to exchange money for a tin can.

The most liquid assets are those assets that contribute to the direct satisfaction of our basic needs. These assets do not need to be exchanged. As soon as there is an exchange, there is a loss of liquidity, however, it is interesting to have assets that can be exchanged, because the more we want a high level of comfort, the more we need others to provide it.

Decorrelation

In traditional finance, decorrelation is the set of management techniques that make it possible to obtain a return on a portfolio of assets that is decorrelated from the return of the financial markets, which is represented by a stock market index. This decorrelation can have two very different objectives: the first objective is to obtain a higher return; the second objective is to protect oneself when the markets fall.

From a survivalist finance perspective, the aim is of course to use decorrelation to protect oneself as best as possible when markets fall and an economic downturn or collapse occurs.

Temporal security

Time is an important element in financial thinking. It is common to think that the more time we have ahead of us, the richer we can become. we may have heard of compound interest, whereby a small amount of money can add up to a large amount of money over a few decades, however, it is better that the interest rates are higher than the inflation rates, otherwise the sum obtained after several decades will be lower in real terms than the sum initially hoarded.

The fact that time favours enrichment is true in a world of economic expansion, not in a world of economic contraction where the more time passes, the more likely it is that economic contraction will eventually hit us.

This is why time does not have the same meaning in the perspective of survivalist finance. Time cannot be seen as a friend that will allow us to get richer and richer, but as a risk for which a certain degree of preparation should be proposed that goes beyond the small precautionary savings that only have value when money has value. We cannot predict exactly when economic collapses may occur.

Time security is the consideration that a certain level of resilience should be ensured as soon as possible, and to do so. To have good temporal security is to have ensured a good level of resilience not for 5 or 10 years from now, but for now.

Resilience-return-risk throuple

The risk-return trade-off is a central concept in traditional finance. The idea is that there is a rule that says that high return goes hand in hand with high risk and that for low risk return can only be low. This is not always true. Pim van Vliet, who has a PhD in finance and is a practitioner of financial markets, has written a book on this subject entitled "High Returns from Low Risk: A Remarkable Stock Market Paradox".

From a survivalist finance perspective, I want to add a third element, resilience, and thus move from a couple to a throuple. I also place this element of resilience even before the two traditional elements.

In the resilience-return-risk throuple, the idea is to invest some of our money in resilience. The proportion of money invested in resilience depends on the level of resilience we want to achieve and the amount of money we want to invest in it. It also depends on our predictions of possible collapse, although we have seen that the concept of time security leads us to believe that economic collapse is best seen as happening now and not in the distant or near future.

CHAPTER 2: SURVIVALIST FINANCE IN A SEDENTARY SITUATION

Survivalist finance in a sedentary situation is focused on the situation of the person who remains in his or her place of living, who is therefore neither nomadic nor has to flee, whatever the reason for the flight. The situation of the nomadic person or the person who has to flee will be considered in the next chapter.

Following the perspective of the resilience-return-risk throuple, I will first focus on the use of money in building resilience and on the development of resilience , then I will discuss financial investment and different assets from a survivalist finance perspective, finally I will discuss bank security and de-banking.

How to achieve a high level of sedentary resilience with little effort and little money

Let us take the 7 fundamental elements that promote survival according to Piero San Giorgio and Vol West (water, food, hygiene and health, energy, knowledge, defence and social link) and add the question of housing.

The aim is to maximise our chances of survival in the event of an economic collapse under the constraint of our laziness and lack of money.

The central idea in meeting this objective is to become self-sufficient in the elements that require little effort and money and to try to find hacks, imperfect shortcuts, for the others.

The choice of home

From a sedentary perspective, this is the most important choice, as it has major consequences in most other pillars of sedentary survival.

The wrong thing to do is to invest one's money in buying a flat or a house in a big city, including suburban areas. The bigger the city, the longer the logistical chains to supply it and the bigger cities are full of unprepared people.

This leaves three options for developing a self-sufficient base: invest in a home that is in a small town, in a village or that is isolated.

Buying an isolated dwelling generally allows us to have a lot of land to produce our own food, but we will see from a survivalist finance perspective that the idea is not necessarily to be self-sufficient in food, because it is complex and time-consuming. Above all, living in isolation means making social contacts more complicated, however, it is easier to survive by having solidarities than by living far from others, and, during an economic collapse, a state, if there is a state left, tends to help the cities more than the countryside, because a revolt in the cities is more dangerous for it because of the mass of the population.

Living in a small town, say around 50,000 inhabitants, can allow us to have a house with a large plot of land, to create solidarity and at the same time to be able to benefit from essential expertise such as the medical expertise that can be found in a small hospital or in specialised private medicine. Living in a small town is Vol West's recommendation, who raises the size of the small town to 100,000 inhabitants.

Living in a village makes it possible to create solidarity, to have a large plot of land, but the expertise of specialist medicine will be difficult to obtain. It is advisable to live in a village where there are one or more general practitioners. Living in a village will cost less than living in a small town.

The choice between the three options depends on our investment capacity, the geographical location we want, especially if we have ties, and the market opportunities.

We will continue to discuss housing choice through the other pillars of survival. One of the consequences of housing choice is what can and cannot be done in terms of water supply.

Water

Water is more important than food, because we can survive for a few weeks without food, but only for a few days without water. We need to drink 1 or 2 litres of water a day on average. Water is also used for cooking and for hygiene.

For our water supply, we are generally dependent on the water that comes through the taps in our homes. Water autonomy answers the question: what would we do if the water stopped coming from the tap?

Being water self-sufficient is relatively easy if we live in a house and own it. By easy, I mean purchasable and quickly set up. If we are a tenant, it is also possible to develop water autonomy if we are in a house, but being a tenant poses important constraints, namely the agreement of the landlord and the fact that we will not own the investments we have made.

There is a great principle in survivalism that says that 1 is 0, 2 is 1, 3 is 2, etc. This means that the means to satisfy a need may be lacking and it is better to have one or more back-up plans.

Depending on the situation, it is possible to obtain water from a spring, a river, a well, a fountain, rain, moisture in the air, a supermarket or a public or private collective system that brings water directly to the tap. Obtaining water from several of these sources is a good way to be self-sufficient in water and to be secure in that autonomy.

Securing water autonomy also involves storage, not being dependent on water supplies, which can be irregular depending on the season, but also on the day and time. Having water stocks allows us to deal with the multiple uses it can have: hydration, washing, use in a possible vegetable garden or for possible farm animals, fire in particular if we are isolated.

There are natural storage facilities: a pond, a lake. There are artificial storage facilities. They can be buried or not. Their volume can be large or small.

For food uses, water needs to be potabilised. This is important because every year several million people die from not drinking safe water (yes, several million). Water can transmit diseases, for example cholera, typhoid, hepatitis or polio. Water can also transmit parasites. This is particularly true in hot climates. Finally, water can be polluted by human production activities, agriculture and industry.

Potabilising water is easy once we have purchased the right technology. All we have to do is buy a gravity filter. The best known is the Berkey filter. Gravity filters remove viruses, bacteria, heavy metals, petroleum products and pesticides. They do not filter out minerals, so it is not possible to obtain demineralised water with a gravity filter. Of course, it is best to always have gravity filters on hand. A properly used, non-failing gravity filter will usually filter just over 10,000 litres of water.

It should be noted that bringing water to the boil sterilises the water, i.e. kills the micro-organisms in the water. This does not solve the problem of heavy metals, petroleum products and pesticides.

Food

We can live for several weeks without eating, however, in order to survive, we need to eat to provide our bodies with sufficient energy to function. This energy varies according to age, sex and physical activity. A soldier who walks 30 km in a day with several dozen kilos on his back will need much more energy, and therefore calories, and therefore food, than an office worker in front of one's computer.

There is, however, one important invariant in all cases: the energy we put into getting our food (and working for a salary or revenues is one of them) must be lastingly lower than the energy our body consumes. The only time we want our body to consume more than we give it is if we want to lose weight.

To use the equations given by Piero San Giorgio and Vol West in their book "Rues barbares" ("Barbaric streets"):

Low energy expenditure + high efficiency = life.

Average energy expenditure + average efficiency = survival.

High energy expenditure + low efficiency = death.

Buy and store

Growing food is extremely complex and time consuming. We think a plant will be well adapted and it is not. The weather or animals can wipe out hundreds of hours of work. While it is possible to reduce the time spent on food production (we will see how in a few pages), there is a much simpler way, which requires little effort and can even save money: buying food and stocking it.

The basic principle is to store what we eat and to eat what we store. It is not a question of storing food and waiting for a break in the supply chain to use it, but of organising a rotation of stocks. It is not a question of storing food that we do not usually eat, but of stocking what we eat, because it will be complicated in a crisis situation to eat something other than what we eat, except for pleasure food if we have larger stocks of pleasure food.

Keep us in mind that with the just-in-time policy, a supermarket only has a few days' supply of food. If there is a logistical problem, for whatever reason, we don't want to be one of those people who will huddle and fight because we do not have a supply.

In addition to the content of the stock, there is the question of how long the stock can last. We now have stocks that can last from a few days to a few weeks. In a survivalist approach, the idea is rather to have a year or even two years of stock.

Stocks depend on the space available and the money that can be invested in them. If we spend 3,000 dollars per year per person on food, this means that building up a year's worth of stocks will cost us about 3,000 dollars.

It is usually written that stocking up saves money because we can buy food in bulk, which can be cheaper, because we can take advantage of discounts and promotions and because stocking up limits the impact of inflation, as buying now is cheaper than buying tomorrow.

It is not always true that stocking up saves money. Imagine that we stockpile for 100 dollars. To save money, we need to save more by stockpiling than we could earn by investing that money.

What is true, however, is that in the long run, storage will allow us to spend less money than if we had bought our food on a day-to-day basis.

One strategy for building up stock is copy-canning. This means buying more of what we already buy when we go to buy. For example, we buy two cans of kidney beans for the week, buy four and store two of the four. Buy a jar of honey for the month? Buy two and store one of the two. When there is a discount or promotion, take full advantage of the discount or promotion. Some supermarkets have cyclical discounts or promotions on the same product. Buy a lot of that product at that time.

Securing stocks

It is not only appropriate to stockpile, we also have to secure the stockpile. Securing involves at least two actions: one, discretion, making sure that stockpiling is not known, unless we live in a village and we are building a resilience system with other members of the village community; and two, making access difficult. A healthy cellar inside a house is a better storage place than a healthy cellar outside the house or inside the house, but with outside access.

Securing stocks does not only mean protecting against thieves, it also means ensuring that stored food will have a good shelf life. What is the point of having a stock if lose it because the food has gone mouldy?

There are many ways to preserve food. Canned food can be either industrially produced or home-made. Salt greatly reduces the moisture content of a food, which deprives micro-organisms that could spoil the food. Sugar and alcohol eliminate bacteria. Oil is also a preservative, but nutritionally it should not be overused. Vinegar preserves a food that is immersed in it due to its acidity. Drying greatly reduces the humidity of a food. Smoking reduces the humidity of a food and covers it with a protective thread. Underground cellars can be used to store fruit and vegetables provided they are left in their original state. Cold winters turn the outside of the house into a natural refrigerator. There is also vacuum packing and owning a fridge or refrigerator, but these are newer and less resilient technologies, especially for the fridge and refrigerator.

Permanent agriculture and the edible forest

Producing food is complex and time-consuming. Usually, it is the last thing we do when we want to develop a self-reliance approach. If we still want to start producing some food, we must keep in mind that there are techniques to reduce the amount of work needed to produce certain types of food. One such technique is the development of an edible forest.

The central idea is to transform an ecosystem to produce food without human intervention, or at least with as little human intervention as possible.

In order to develop an edible forest, it is necessary to understand what food species grow naturally in the place where we live. For example, in the area where I grew up, there were many chestnut trees. Personally, I like to eat roasted chestnuts and from a nutritional point of view chestnuts have great advantages: they have a high caloric value (180 kilocalories per 100 grams), a lot of fibre, are rich in starch, etc.

Developing an edible forest means helping native food species to have a larger share in the forest. This may mean, for example, replanting a beautiful new chestnut tree that was unlucky enough to be born in the wrong place to a more suitable location, or introducing a perennial that is not in the original forest, but which will thrive there without human help. In some cases this might be wild garlic, which is a shade-loving species. An edible forest is different from an orchard. For an orchard to last, a lot of human work is needed, because the orchard does not fit naturally into the functioning of nature. It is the opposite of an edible forest.

If we want to go further into the issues of food production, I recommend books on permaculture, gathering, fishing, hunting and trapping.

Hygiene and health

The question of hygiene is an easily solved one. Soap is needed for body hygiene and washing powder for clothing hygiene. Soap and detergent can be stocked and it is possible to make our own soap and detergent.

Soap is made from caustic soda and oil, which can be replaced by animal fat if oil is not available. Soap making is based on a chemical reaction, saponification. Saponification is a chemical reaction between two components: a fat (oil or butter of vegetable or animal origin) and soda (solid soap making) or potash (liquid soap making). Cold saponification can be done at home.

There are different ways to make laundry: use soap, use soap with baking soda, use ash, use ivy.

The issue of health is infinitely more complex. It takes almost a decade for a student to become a medical doctor. There are dozens of medical specialties. Hundreds of billions of dollars are invested every year in medical research in the public and private sectors. But in a world of economic collapse, health services can also collapse.

Five decisions can be made about health to increase resilience. The first decision is to have a stock of basic medicines and a stock of instruments and care products. When we need drug X from this stock, we take the oldest drug X in the stock and buy a new drug X. The principle is the same as for food, "consume what we store and store what we consume", except that medicines are not food, we cannot produce them ourself and unless we have a health problem we do not take a medicine regularly.

The second decision is to create a stock of medicines related to the pathologies that we may have.

The third decision is to buy books on medicine when experiencing shortage as well as other medical and herbal books. Here is a list of books that are useful to have at home:

- "Where there is no doctor. A Village Health Care Handbook". David Werner describes what can be done in health care without a doctor and with few resources. The book is in its 18ème edition when I am writing these words.

- "Where there is no dentist". Murray Dickson describes what can be done about dental care without a dentist and with few resources. The book is in its 13ème edition.

- "When There Is No Doctor: Preventive and Emergency Healthcare in Uncertain Times. Gerard Doyle offers another book on medicine without a medical doctor and with few resources.

- For those who appreciate alternative medicine, it can be interesting to have some books on the subject.

WARNING: as long as we have access to a medical doctor or a nurse, we should always go through them. A book will never replace a person who has studied for several years, and for a medical doctor, it is almost 10 years of study!

The fourth decision, if possible, is to move to a village or small town where there are medical doctors. If there is an economic collapse, there will be a shortage of medicines and medical devices, but as long as the doctors are alive, the knowledge they have learned will exist and they will be able to pass it on to us.

If you are young, thinking about preparing for a collapse, and medicine appeals to you, maybe working to become a medical doctor would be a good idea.

This brings us to the fifth decision. If we do not want to become a medical doctor or are too old to become one, we can take some courses, including first aid.

Energy

Energy is essential for at least two reasons. The first is to avoid dying from the cold or its consequences in countries with cold seasons. The second is that energy provides material comfort by allowing for example the use of light, household appliances, a computer, the internet, a telephone, etc.

There are many, many sources of energy, and not all these sources can meet all types of energy needs. For example, we cannot run a computer on a wood fire, even though wood is the most traditional source of energy for heating and cooking.

A distinction should be made between primary and secondary energy. Secondary energy is energy obtained by transforming primary energy. For example, electricity is a secondary energy that can be obtained by transforming various primary energies such as nuclear energy, hydraulics, oil, wind power or solar energy.

Heating

The first way to keep warm is to conserve the heat that our body produces. So it is all about clothing. I was lucky enough to live in a country with a freezing winter for a year and when it came to getting out of overheated buildings, I did what everyone else did: I put on layers and layers of clothes.

The second way to heat is to have a passive house. This means having a house that captures as much energy as possible in winter and conserves it.

The third way to heat is to use cooking for heating. When we heat food, we also heat the home. In the same way, the use of electrical equipment, such as a computer or a light bulb, contributes to the heating of the dwelling, even if the heat released is low.

The fourth way of heating is to install a heating system in the house. This heating can be powered by various energy sources: wood, oil, nuclear, hydraulic, wind, solar, etc. The best is to use an energy source in which we can be autonomous and for this wood is the best option. It is enough to have a small forest to be autonomous in firewood.

With global warming, getting rid of heat will become increasingly important. Air conditioning reduces autonomy and promotes global warming in the long term, but also in the moment, since the air conditioning process only transfers heat from inside to outside, raising the outside temperature. In the countryside this has no effect, but it does have an effect in the city, where temperatures are already warmer than in the countryside. There are different ways to reduce heat and hot countries are a good model for ideas to reduce heat in hot seasons, but it is clear that houses that have healthy underground parts will become more and more attractive.

Generating electricity

Electricity can be generated from a variety of primary energy sources, however, before thinking about generating electricity, it is important to understand what our electricity needs are and whether it is possible to reduce them so that we need to generate less.

Stand-alone means of generating electricity are mainly solar panels, wind turbines and generators, which are usually powered by fuel.

Electricity must be stored, as there is no match between instantaneous production and instantaneous consumption of electricity. The storage of electricity requires technological means such as batteries, inverters and voltage converters. Batteries are used to store energy. An inverter is used to provide temporary power in the event of a power cut. It is also used to give certain electrical appliances such as computers the precise voltage they need. A voltage converter transforms the DC voltage delivered by the batteries into the AC voltage supplied by the electricity grid.

Knowledge

Knowledge is infinite or almost infinite, but some knowledge is more useful than others, because it is used more frequently or responds to emergencies. This is why it is more important to focus on knowledge that promotes autonomy and knowledge that responds to emergencies.

The main knowledge hack is to build a library so that we have the books at home in case we need them. Of course, it is better to read them bit by bit than to admire the binding, but having them at home without having read them is better than not having read them and not having them.

What do we find in our survivalist library? First, books that help to survive in uncertain and difficult times, i.e. books on food production and storage, cooking, water, hygiene, medical and health, energy, psychology, barter economy, etc. Second, books that offer recreation. On this point, it is also interesting to have games that allow us to enjoy ourself (checkers, chess, board games, etc.), especially if we have children.

Defence

Defence includes the defence of ourselves, our loved ones and our assets, especially those important to our resilience and survival.

There is no such thing as absolute security. It is not possible to guard against all attacks, however, there are some basic ideas to be aware of:

- Not to be noticed for ostentatious signs of wealth

- Not to be noticed for our behaviour

- Not behave as a victim or as an aggressor

- Avoid conflict, avoid confrontation, which requires being able to ignore our ego in many situations

- Be harder to steal

- Be harder to attack

- Be harder to kill

Generally speaking, for a robbery, assault or crime to occur, three conditions must be met:

- An individual capable of committing the offence or intent on committing an offence

- An attractive target

- A relatively unprotected target

Let us look a little more closely at how we can reduce the likelihood of being robbed or assaulted.

The concept of the 'grey man

The concept of the 'grey man' refers to the behaviours that one should adopt to reduce the likelihood of getting into trouble. The basic idea is to have behaviours that anonymise us, that blend us into the mass. This anonymisation takes different forms: anonymisation in the clothes we wear, in the physical environment we create, in the emotions we show, in the words we say, etc.

More precisely, our clothes are in line with other people's clothes, not only the shapes and colours, but also the wear. No jewellery, nothing shiny, forget about luxury watches[1] .

No distinctive smell. we wash if everyone else washes. we stink if everyone stinks. We pay attention to kitchen smells (and kitchen noises) if no one is cooking. No noise. If there is noise, it is to hide another noise that is important to hide. We pay cash as much as possible, at least when it comes to developing autonomy.

If everyone is hungry, then we have to act as if we are hungry, even if we have been foresighted compared to others. If everyone is crying, then we cry. We run when everyone else is running and we walk when everyone else is walking.

One only talks about one's self-sufficient base project with trustworthy people, i.e. people who will keep the information to themselves and who are useful for the project or whom one wishes to be able to protect.

Passive home defence

Losing control of one's home means losing the level of autonomy that this control allows us as well as the physical and psychological security that it provides.

The first passive defence of the home is not to give others the desire to take possession of it. This is why the home

---

[1] Unless we are a nomad with a particular situation, which we will see in the section on survivalist finance in a nomadic situation.

should not show any signs of affluence, including inside, and why it is best to make it difficult to see what is inside.

The second passive home defence is to create natural barriers to the home by fences, thorny bushes and hedges. We can even do double duty by choosing thorny bushes and hedges that provide food, such as mulberry trees. It may also be worthwhile to use gravel to hear footsteps and to make it easier for our dog to sound the alarm if we have one.

The third passive defence of the home is to reinforce all the elements that allow entry into the home: the door, of course, but also windows, French windows, sliding doors, etc. For example, we can have a reinforced door and a reinforced wall, shutters that close from the inside, etc. For example, we can have an armoured door and a reinforced wall, shutters that close from the inside, etc.

In general, it is a good idea to put ourself in the position of a possible burglar and ask ourself how to break into the house in order to detect problems in the security of our home.

We should make sure, however, that we can get out of our home through different exits, for example in case of fire. In this respect, it is important to have a sufficient number of up-to-date, functional fire extinguishers.

Finally, we should choose a room in the house that will serve as a refuge in case of an intruder and as a place to activate the active defence in case of a threat to our life and the lives of our family.

Active defence (of oneself, one's family and the home)

The use of active defence opens the question of self-defence. You have to know the law of the country in which you live. I am in France when I write these words and in French law, the conditions for self-defence are explained in Article 122-5 of the Penal Code. It is this article that provides the legal framework for the use of active defence in France.

Article 122-5 of the French Penal Code reads:

"A person, who faced with an unjustified attack on oneself or another and at the same time performs an act required for the legitimate defence of oneself or another, shall not be criminally liable, unless the means of defence employed are disproportionate to the gravity of the attack.

A person who, in order to interrupt the execution of a crime or offence against property, performs an act of defence, other than voluntary manslaughter, is not criminally liable when this act is strictly necessary for the purpose pursued, provided that the means employed are proportionate to the seriousness of the offence."

There are different types of weapons: firearms, bladed and non-lethal weapons, improvised weapons, martial arts. In all cases, if we are in a situation that requires the use of active defence, the basic principle is that we must win.

Personally, I am not a fan of firearms. I think the risk of accident is too great for the benefit, even in a state like France that uses armed police to maim protesters.

One can see, however, that what matters is not the fact that many people own guns, but the gun culture in the different countries. There are countries where there are many guns and few crimes and accidents (I think of Switzerland), there are also countries where there are both many guns and many crimes and accidents (I think of the USA). Guns are not bad or good as such. When they are allowed, the quality of their use and non-use depends on the culture of the country and the people.

Collective defence

The elements given above are intended to help improve personal defence on an essentially individual level, however, we are infinitely stronger in a group than we are alone. A tight-knit group of people is stronger than one person alone. Developments in recent decades have broken up families and groups, but history has left impressive traces of the collective capacity for defence. In ancient times, for example, underground "cities" were built to protect themselves from external aggression, with room for tens of thousands of people. This is the case, for example, of the underground "city" of Derinkuyu in Cappadocia (Turkey).

I also think that in the event of an economic collapse, it is interesting that an active defence could be organised at the level of a village, a district or a town, and this active defence could be a rotating active defence so that everyone does their bit. This is the idea defended by Yves Cochet, a former French minister of ecology, in his conception of active security in a situation of economic collapse.

Social link

Why social ties are essential for survival

Imagine we have a very well equipped self-sufficient base and we produce our own food. we are self-sufficient, but we are only self-sufficient until something in our system breaks down and we are not able to fix it. At that point, we will have to live without that component. For example, if it is a piece of the electrical system, then we will have to live without electricity. If it is our last water filter, then we will not be able to filter our water and make it drinkable. Even if we are self-sufficient, we are dependent on some of society's outputs, and giving up a lot of comfort does not change the reality of this fact, even if it reduces the scale of it.

The social link allows us a certain specialisation and solidarity. Specialisation allows us to build a more productive economy and therefore better comfort. Although there are cases of people who have lived in total autarky, these cases are rare, the life they have had has been more than rustic and there are few people who would accept to live such a life. Solidarity also helps to cope with hard times and provides security from the outside world.

Psychology of the social link

Here are three basic principles of human psychology of social bonding, three principles to facilitate the creation of social bonding with our environment.

The first principle is not to wait for the neighbours to make the first move. we have to do it ourself. The reason is simple: if everyone waits, nothing will happen. Moreover, as we are in the process of building our resilience, we have an interest in making something happen.

The second principle is the principle of reciprocity. There has to be a certain balance between what we give and what we receive. We cannot receive forever, just as we cannot give forever. This is a universal norm, but there are individual differences. Some people respect the principle of reciprocity more than others and some forget it. It is also worth asking what it is for oneself, knowing that we may tend to overestimate our respect for the principle, and what it is for the people around us. Another inter-individual difference is that some people are more likely to respond positively to a positive act and others (or the same) to respond negatively to a negative act.

The third principle is that there must be a good reason to make another person experience a negative emotion. There are scientific studies that have been done on negative emotions and positive emotions. We have to experience a lot of positive emotions in order to get rid of a negative emotion.

Financial investment from the perspective of survivalist finance

It is possible to focus solely on building resilience, just as it is possible to consider that building resilience is only the primary response to the risk of economic collapse, and that it is possible to build assets to support this resilience.

It is also possible to consider that an economic collapse is a possible scenario, but that there is also the scenario where there is no economic collapse and that we should prepare for a possible economic collapse and enjoy our short life in a world without collapse.

Here we will look at the different assets according to the purpose they serve. The asset categories are resilience assets, defence assets, anti-fragile assets, performance assets and growth assets. It should be noted that within this typology, an asset can belong to different asset categories, as it can fulfil several purposes. The weighting of assets in the portfolio depends on the goals to be achieved.

Resilience assets

Resilience assets are the assets which enable people to be empowered in meeting their needs. In other words, they are all the assets we have just seen in the previous section on ways of building a high level of resilience.

It is worth bearing in mind that most wealthy people do not, at the time of writing, have wealth that is resilient to an economic collapse. At best, they will have wealth that incorporates defensive assets. If we have built up our resilience assets, we are already richer than most rich people in the event of an economic collapse.

Defence assets

Defence assets are investments in economic activities that either meet basic needs for which we are not self-sufficient, or needs for which we are self-sufficient, but for which we wish to create a different line of defence than self-sufficiency. In other words, defence assets are mainly basic products and medical products.

The first case, investing in economic activities that meet basic needs for which we are not self-sufficient, is by far the most important from the perspective of survivalist finance. It is about seeking protection in essential areas where we do not have it.

A first example is investing in a company that makes canned food in order to have a piece of the company in case there is an economic situation that makes it difficult to get food. Having a piece of the business provides at least partial protection against price inflation. If it is a small business in which we are a major investor, the business can even become a direct source of supply.

Another example is the pharmaceutical industry. If drug prices are rising, then having investments in pharmaceutical companies is a way of partially hedging one's bets in the hope that the gains from the investments can reduce the impact of inflation on drug prices. From an autonomous perspective, it is quite possible to develop one's own medicinal plant garden or to develop mutual support relationships with people who have created their own garden, however, not everything can be treated with medicinal herbs. Let us remember that before the Industrial Revolution it took two children to make an adult to use the word of the historian Pierre Goubert, because one in two children died before becoming an adult.

The second case, investing in economic activities that meet needs where we are self-sufficient, is much less important, but if it is financially possible, it is a way of creating a second line of defence in case we lose part of our self-sufficiency in meeting a need and having invested in this type of asset can be a relief. In general, it is also worth considering that if we are in a survivalist financial mode, this is not the case for everyone, including most rich people.

In any case, it should be noted that states tend to be more interventionist in the event of a crisis in meeting people's basic needs. There is a natural incentive for this interventionism: the desire to avoid revolts and, above all, revolutions, however, protecting oneself with defence assets means that one is not waiting for the state to act, which is an act of empowerment.

Some assets may be between resilience and defence assets. For example, if we buy a farm and rent part of it to an agroecology-oriented farmer, the most important objective is not the rent he or she can pay, but the fact that we have an important skill nearby in case of an economic collapse. That is why in such a situation it is more interesting to rent well below the market price in order to help this farmer develop one's activity and expertise rather than looking for a financial return.

Antifragile assets

The concept of antifragility was developed by Nassim Nicholas Taleb in his book "Antifragile: Things that Gain from Disorder". Fragility occurs when a system suffers from the variability of its environment beyond a certain threshold. Antifragility is the fact that a system benefits from the variability of its environment. The concept of antifragility is fundamentally different from the concept of resilience, which is the ability to cope with a difficult situation.

Applied to finance, the principle of antifragility means that an antifragile asset increases in value when other assets fall in value. For example, gold is generally an antifragile asset because its price tends to rise during crises, while most assets tend to fall.

In the recent past, Google's shares have behaved antifragile, while Apple's shares have not, however, both companies are technology companies and therefore their shares can neither be considered as resilience assets nor even as defence assets.

Resilience assets and defensive assets can be antifragile in crisis situations, but this is not a rule. In the COVID crisis, for example, we saw that commodity prices fell as economic activity fell. Commodities as assets did not prove to be antifragile in this crisis, whereas in other crises they may have been. An asset can be antifragile in one crisis... and fragile in another. The antifragility of an asset depends on the type of crisis experienced. The COVID crisis favoured technological companies, a shortage of energy resources due to decades of wasted energy resources could refocus the economy on meeting basic needs and thus wipe out technological companies.

From a survivalist finance perspective, however, it may be interesting to cross-reference the issue of resilience assets and defence assets with the issue of antifragility. A defensive asset that is antifragile during an economic collapse may be more attractive than a defensive asset that is not.

Performance assets

Performance assets are assets for which generous dividends are paid. They are part of a traditional wealth strategy. They are only interesting from a survivalist finance perspective for the part of the wealth that is not part of a survivalist perspective.

Growth assets

Growth assets are assets that are expected to increase in value significantly. The purpose of these assets is to increase wealth more quickly. They are part of a traditional wealth strategy. They are only interesting from a survivalist financial perspective for the part of the wealth that is not part of a survivalist perspective.

Non-Ponzi crypto-assets are growth assets, as the investment objective is to take a share in a project that is expected to grow and provide a strong increase in the value of the crypto-asset. Note, however, that due to the lack of regulation, strong project-based crypto-assets are riskier growth assets than shares in start-ups that have raised their funds in the traditional way.

The same asset can belong to several asset classes

In the typology presented, the same asset can belong to several categories. Let's take a property. It can be a resilience asset if it fosters our autonomy, a defence asset if it is rented to a farmer practising agroecology, an antifragile asset if its real price tends to rise during crises, a yield asset if it allows us to have a nice rent every month compared to the costs it generates, and a growth asset if real estate prices are rising very fast.

Bank security and de-banking

The question of security is at the heart of the choices of banking and de-banking. When one has an account with a bank or more generally a financial institution, the bank or financial institution has a responsibility to ensure the security of that account, however, the downside of this security is that our assets can be frozen or the bank or financial institution can fail and make us lose all or part of our assets. When we have assets that are de-banked, such as crypto-assets or luxury items, we are responsible for their security.

One way of providing security in banking security is to be in two or more banks in two or more countries. It is about having banking diversification. This is generally not illegal vis-à-vis the tax authorities, provided that they are informed, however, the countries and banks must be chosen carefully. The countries should have a long history of respect for property rights and the banks should have a track record and policy that protects them from bankruptcy and fraud.

Note that having several banks allows us to have several bank cards, which can be useful if a card is blocked for technical reasons.

To provide more security, it is also possible to have part of one's assets unbanked. Being partially unbanked can be part of a banking diversification strategy, except that the additional bank is ourselves.

Being fully or largely de-banked means being responsible for the security of our assets, not just for a part of our assets, but on all or most of our assets. If there is a security problem, this can be an extremely complicated situation. While it may be difficult to have a real estate asset stolen, unless it is stolen by a state, it may be possible to have a crypto wallet stolen, including one protected by a physical wallet. This is why a mix of bank diversification and de-banking is probably the most secure approach.

CHAPTER 3: SURVIVALIST FINANCE IN NOMADIC OR FLIGHT SITUATIONS

In this chapter, we will look at the particular perspective of survivalist finance for two types of people who have different lives but have the same need: to be mobile.

These two types of people are:

- People who wish to prepare themselves to be able to flee their place of residence or even their country if necessary

- People who have adopted a nomadic lifestyle.

Many elements that are valid in a sedentary situation are also valid in a nomadic or flight situation. For example, the asset typology remains effective, as do the ideas of banking security, however, nomadic resilience has its own peculiarities and, above all, is much more complicated than sedentary resilience.

The difficulties of modern nomadic resilience

To fully understand the difficulties of nomadic resilience in an industrialised world, it is first necessary to understand how classical nomads lived and still live.

Traditionally, there are several types of nomadic peoples: nomadic hunting or fishing peoples, nomadic peoples of pastoral societies and peripatetic nomadic peoples. Among nomadic hunting and fishing peoples, the alternation of resources and seasons dictates movement. These peoples are in constant search of food. In North America, for example, the Indians of the boreal forest alternate between hunting in winter and fishing in summer. During the hunting season, they follow the buffalo and caribou herds.

Nomadic peoples in pastoral societies are generally on land where agriculture is not possible. The domestication of livestock has allowed their societies to be organised around the ownership of livestock. The Mongols, who live on the cold steppes of Central Asia, are among the nomadic peoples who practice pastoral livestock.

Peripatetic nomadic peoples are peoples who move among sedentary populations offering a craft or trade. The Roma are the best known to Europeans, but there are many others worldwide: in India there are about thirty peripatetic nomadic peoples, in Iran more than twenty.

Traditional nomadic peoples have associated nomadism with a way of obtaining the goods necessary for their survival. Nomadic hunting and fishing peoples and nomadic peoples in pastoral societies are self-consuming, whereas peripatetic nomadic peoples trade goods or services in order to survive, making them dependent not directly on nature, but on the sedentary peoples among whom they live.

Modern nomads and people fleeing a dramatic situation such as war are closer to peripatetic nomadic peoples than to nomadic hunting or fishing peoples and nomadic peoples in pastoral societies: they are not in a situation where they produce what they consume, but where they depend on their relationship with those among whom they live to be able to live. A high level of resilience means producing as much as possible of what we consume or having stocks of what we do not produce to have some visibility in a future which is by nature uncertain.

How do we build resilience when we are a modern nomad, or when we think we may one day have to flee the place where we live? There is unfortunately no miracle solution to achieve the degree of resilience of a sedentary person with a survivalist approach to finance. It is necessary to create a refuge (or several), i.e. a place that will not be as good as a real self-sufficient base, but that would allow us to hold on in a world that is economically collapsing. Let us take a closer look at the different forms a shelter can take so that we can see which type of shelter is best suited to our personal and family situation and our financial means.

The shelter(s)

The fundamental difference between a sedentary and a nomadic situation lies in the impossibility of storing large quantities (water, food, tools, medicines, books in paper format, firewood, etc.) and creating strong social links with the people living around us on a daily basis.

Hence the interest in creating one or more shelters.

Here are four types of shelters, from best to worst.

The first type of shelter, which is the most successful, is to have a mini self-sufficient mini base, for example a small house with land in the countryside or in a small town, which is self-sufficient in water and electricity, in which one has a stove for wood heating, wood reserves, food reserves and some basic medicines. Each year, one spends several times a year living in this house to maintain it, to run the stocks and to make friends with the neighbours. It will not be as good as a real self-sufficient base where one lives permanently or almost permanently, but it is better than what most people have.

A second type of shelter is to have a shelter in the home of a trusted person, usually a family member. We can help them to partially transform their home into a self-sufficient base, for example by contributing to the costs of making the home self-sufficient in electricity, water or heating, or by developing a food stock in their home that is in line with their (and our) tastes, which they can then run.

A third type of shelter is to have a converted truck with some electricity, food and water for several days. The advantage of such a truck, coupled with the fact of having sufficient fuel cans in reserve, is to be able to quickly flee an emergency situation to go to a nearby country and then have a roof over one's head, regardless of the help that may be found later on. Note that the heavier a vehicle is, the more fuel is needed to travel the same number of kilometres. The weight of a vehicle is the primary factor in fuel consumption. This must be considered. By the way, this type of shelter is in itself a home for those who live the so-called "van life".

A fourth type of shelter is to have a storehouse in a warehouse (or in the home of a trusted person). This can be used to store food, medicine and goods, e.g. water purifiers, clothes, etc. The concern with food stocks is that it is complicated to rotate them here.

Assets and geographical freedom

Owning assets of any kind promotes geographical freedom. Indeed, owning assets provides a store of value and can bring returns. This is the case for shares when dividends are paid or for real estate when it is rented[1].

When assets provide a sufficiently high return, it is possible to live without working. If not, they provide a kind of insurance, they can provide a living for a while when the entrepreneurial activity does not generate enough money or it takes a little too long to find a new job.

Owning assets promotes freedom as long as property rights are respected. We have seen recently that states that seemed secure in respecting property rights have challenged those property rights to silence opponents or to discriminate against citizens of another state on the basis that being a citizen of that state was considered to mean supporting the state's policies.

While all assets can support geographical freedom, not all assets have the same value from a nomadic perspective and

---

[1] By the way, it might seem strange to say that owning a property promotes geographical freedom, but it is quite possible to delegate the management of a property against a loss of profitability due to the payment of property management services.

certain characteristics should be sought whether or not one is nomadic.

The first characteristic to look for is to have an asset that is secure in terms of property rights. Recent events in Canada during the protests against the vaccine policy and more generally in the West during the Russian intervention in Ukraine have shown that even in countries where property rights were thought to be best protected, they are not. All it takes is the wrong political ideas, depending on the power or nationality, for this property right to be violated.

There are at least two principles to follow to address this problem. The first is to consider that any country that has not respected property rights in the past is a country that will not respect them in the future. This does not mean not investing in that country, this means that if we invest we should take into account in the investment risks the fact that the country may violate property rights. The second principle is to diversify geographically in order to reduce dependence on the political decisions of a single country.

Diversifying geographically means two things: first, investing in different countries; and second, having the investments go through intermediaries from different countries. If we only have an intermediary or intermediaries that are legally dependent on one country and that country asks the intermediary or intermediaries to block our assets, then we lose access to those assets. we do not just have to diversify the countries we invest in, we have to diversify the nationality of the intermediaries.

The second characteristic to look for is to have assets in the currencies we use. Imagine that we only travel to countries that use the dollar and that your assets are only in countries that do not use the dollar. If the dollar falls against other currencies, your financial situation improves, but if the dollar rises, the opposite happens. Investing in assets denominated in currencies other than the ones we use to buy the goods and services we need for our lives creates an additional risk which is called currency risk. This is why it is important that some of the assets we own are denominated in the currency or currencies we use most in our daily lives.

The third characteristic to look for is the liquidity of assets in the traditional sense. An asset is said to be liquid when it can be bought or sold quickly without this having a strong influence on its price. It is not necessary for all the assets one owns to be liquid, but it is important that some of them are so that they can be sold quickly in the event of a risk to property rights, the need to flee or a rapid fall in price.

A fourth feature could have been the ability to buy and sell at a distance, but in some countries it is even possible to buy and sell a good remotely. This is particularly the case in countries, where procedures can be dematerialised if necessary, however, buying a property remotely can generate risks, as one buys on the basis of plans, photos or videos and not after one or more careful visits.

In the case of preparing for a flight scenario, whatever the reason for the flight, the idea is to have at least one flight country and assets in it. It is then possible to allocate assets from the perspective of survivalist finance in a sedentary situation with a primacy given to resilience assets and defence assets, or even antifragile assets.

In the case of simple nomadism, it is also interesting to give primacy to resilience assets and defence assets, or even anti-fragile assets.

Survivalist crypto-assets

The world of crypto-assets is marked by a culture of freedom from institutions, especially financial institutions. This culture of freedom is also shared by modern nomads. This is why crypto-assets have a special part in the relationship between assets and geographical freedom.

At the heart of survivalist crypto, i.e. the relationship between crypto-assets and survivalism, are two questions. One, how do we use crypto-assets to survive? Two, how do we survive in the crypto world?

How to use crypto-assets to survive? Some crypto-assets are also called crypto-currencies. A traditional currency has three functions: it can be a unit of account, a store of value and a medium for exchange.

From a survivalist perspective, we are interested in the function of a store of value and the function of a medium for exchange. The more crypto-assets are used for purchasing purposes, the more interesting they are as a medium for exchange. Crypto-assets can be used as a store of value, however, their volatility makes them a risky store of value, especially since when using a crypto-asset as a medium for exchange, exchanges are calculated in a traditional currency and then converted into the crypto-asset taking into account the evolution of its parity with the traditional currency, which creates an exchange risk.

Crypto-assets, however, have a function that traditional currencies cannot fulfil, they provide additional security, the security that comes from being disconnected from state currencies that states can use in liberticidal projects such as controlling their population.

How to survive in the crypto world? The crypto world is a very volatile world, i.e. very risky. The prices of crypto-assets can vary greatly in a short period of time. The classic strategy to protect ourself is to try to take advantage of prolonged moments of rising prices ("bull market") and spend a large part of our crypto portfolio in stablecoins, which are crypto assets backed by traditional currencies, or get out of crypto during prolonged moments of falling prices ("bear market").

As the crypto world develops, one can imagine that increasingly complex strategies found in traditional markets will be put in place, for example derivatives that allow us to make money with crypto-assets whose prices fall.

Crossing a border with a lot of money

Being nomadic or fleeing often means crossing borders. It is possible to cross borders with a lot of money and little weight. First, there is the fact of having crypto-assets on one's physical wallet(s) of cryto-assets or "hard wallets" (or not, but this is not recommended for security reasons). There is also the fact of having on one's person light objects that have a lot of value: luxury watches, luxury pens, jewellery (especially signet rings for men), gold coins, precious stones, etc.

Reporting requirements vary from country to country, however, it should be noted that states are gradually adapting to practices in order to combat terrorist financing and tax evasion.

Thus, for EU countries, the concept of cash includes banknotes, bearer negotiable instruments, anonymous prepaid electronic cards and goods used as a store of highly liquid value (gems, watches, gold, etc.).

As far as crypto-assets are concerned, it all depends on how they are used. If it's about using our crypto-assets to finance our daily life in a foreign country like we do with an international bank card, then it shouldn't be a problem, however, if it involves moving large sums of money from one country to another in order to avoid paying taxes, then this could be considered tax evasion. It should also be noted that some countries ban the use of crypto-assets and others restrict their use. In 2021, a report by the Global Legal Research Directorate (GLRD), which is a department of the US Library of Congress, listed 51 countries that restrict the flow of cryptocurrencies.

The purchase of a golden passport

Not all nationalities are purchasable. In many countries, it takes several years of legal residence before the nationality can be acquired, however, some nationalities are purchasable. This means that if we pay a certain amount of money or invest a certain amount of money in a country, then we get the nationality of that country. The so-called golden passport is a proof of the acquisition of nationality.

Buying another nationality can serve three purposes:

- live in a more stable and protective country than our own

- be able to flee to another country if there is a problem in our own country, for example war or civil war

- travel more freely, either because the new passport allows us to travel to more countries, or because it allows to travel more easily to some countries that the first passport does not.

It does not matter if we buy a passport to achieve one of these three objectives. As soon as we buy a passport, we can achieve all three.

If one wants to buy a nationality, one has to check before one buys the nationality that the country of our nationality allows citizens to have more than one nationality. There are countries that do not allow their citizens to have more than one nationality.

Strong countries do not allow people the purchase of nationality. The purchase of nationality is generally allowed by small countries, however, for people who are not nationals of an European Union country, it is possible to buy a European Union passport by purchasing Maltese citizenship.

For EU nationals, only a small country sells its nationality and it usually costs 100,000 dollars or more to buy it. The list of these countries changes over time: some countries stop selling their nationality and others start selling it.

The sale of nationality is not new. St Kitts and Nevis in the Caribbean has had a "citizenship by investment" scheme since 1984.

CONCLUSION

59

If the book has taught you at least one good idea, then it has been useful. I hope, however, that it has taught you a lot more!